Queen Arthur

Nicola Prentis

Queen Arthur
by Nicola Prentis

Burlington Books
P.O. Box 54411
3721 Limassol
Cyprus
Burlington Books is an imprint of the Burlington Group.

The publisher gratefully acknowledges the following:
© CD Bank / Jupiter Images: page 50 (c); © Getty Images / PhotoDisc: pages 7 (f), 34 (4), 50 (b); © Photos.com / Jupiter Images: pages 7 (e), 20 (2); © Shutterstock,Inc: cover, pages 6, 7 (a, b, c, d, g, h, i), 12, 13 (all except 2), 28, 34 (all except 4), 42, 50 (all except b, c), 56, 57, 58, 59

The publisher would like to thank the following people:
Castellano:	Alicia Ruiz Cuéllar
Català:	Maria Esteve Serraviñals
Euskara:	Edurne Azkue Urrestilla
Galego:	Ramón Nicolás Rodríguez

All rights reserved by the publisher. No part of this publication may be reproduced, stored in a retrieval system or transmitted in any form or by any means – electronic, mechanical, photocopying or otherwise – without permission in writing from the publisher.

ISBN 978-9925-30-157-7
Copyright © 2018 Burlington Books
Burlington Reader No. NE2.17
Print run: 5/24

CONTENTS

Introduction	4
Chapter 1: Trapped!	8
Chapter 2: A Shock for Gwen	10
Chapter 3: Just Like in the Stories	14
Chapter 4: A Hard Lesson for Arthur	16
Chapter 5: King Arthur Goes to Camelot	22
Chapter 6: A Surprising Visitor	25
Chapter 7: A Terrible Dragon	30
Chapter 8: A Dangerous Situation	32
Chapter 9: A Conversation Between Two Friends	36
Chapter 10: Hard to Be a Girl	39
Chapter 11: The Sword in the Stone	44
Chapter 12: The End of the Problem	47
Epilogue	49
Glossary	52
Cross-Curricular Focus	56

Introducción

Gwen, una chica de 15 años, está huyendo de sus acosadoras cuando se ve atrapada en un callejón sin salida. Allí se topa con una roca que tiene una barra metálica clavada. Cuando la saca, descubre que es una espada mágica que la ha transportado al pasado, a los días previos a la coronación del rey Arturo. El joven Arturo, que estuvo a punto de extraerla, está furioso con Gwen porque sea ella la que tenga que cumplir la profecía en vez de él. Disfrazada de chico, Gwen se convierte en rey, pero ¿el arrogante Arturo aceptará ser su escudero? ¿Y Gwen se escapará de la malvada bruja Morgana y del terrible dragón cuando se encuentre frente a ellos?

Introducció

La Gwen, una noia de 15 anys, està fugint de les seves assetjadores quan es veu atrapada en un carreró sense sortida. Allà troba una barra metàl·lica clavada en una roca. Quan la treu, descobreix que és una espasa màgica que l'ha traslladat al passat, als dies previs a la coronació del rei Artur. El jove Artur, que va estar a punt de treure l'espasa, està furiós amb la Gwen perquè ara és ella qui ha de complir la profecia en lloc d'ell. La Gwen esdevé rei, disfressada de noi, però l'arrogant Artur acceptarà ser el seu escuder? I la Gwen s'escaparà de la malvada bruixa Morgana i del terrible drac quan se'ls trobi?

Sarrera

Gwen, 15 urteko neskatoa, kale itsu batean harrapatuta gelditu da, erasotzaileengandik ihesi doala. Eta han, haitz batean iltzatuta, metalezko barra bat aurkitu du. Atera duenean, iraganera eraman duen ezpata magikoa dela ohartu da, Artur Erregearen koroatze aurreko egunetara. Ezpata ia-ia ateratzea lortu zuen Artur gaztea Gwenekin haserre dago, neskatoa delako, eta ez bera, profezia beteko duena. Mutil mozorrotuta, Gwen errege bilakatu da, baina onartuko ote du Artur harroputzak bere ezkutari izatea? Eta ihes egiterik izango ote du Gwenek Morgana sorgin gaiztoarengandik eta herensuge izugarriarengandik, aurrez aurre topo egiten dutenean?

Limiar

Gwen, unha rapaza de 15 anos, está a fuxir das súas acosadoras cando se ve atrapada nunha canella sen saída. Alí se atopa cunha rocha que ten unha barra metálica cravada. Ao sacala, descobre que é unha espada máxica que a transportou ao pasado, aos días previos á coroación do rei Artur. O mozo Artur, que estivo a piques de extraela, está furioso con Gwen porque sexa ela a que teña que cumprir a profecía no canto del. Baixo o disfrace de rapaz, Gwen convértese en rei, mais…, o arrogante Artur aceptará ser o seu escudeiro? E Gwen fuxirá da malvada bruxa Morgana e do terríbel dragón cando se atope diante deles?

THE CHARACTERS

Gwen

Arthur

Merlin

Morgana

PRE-READING ACTIVITIES

1 Look at the pictures connected to the story. Then match the words to the pictures.

1. stone
2. wizard
3. fields
4. king
5. smoke
6. lake
7. castle
8. cave

a

b

c

d

e

f

g

h

2 Look at the pictures again. Do you think this is a true story or a fantasy? Explain your answers.

....

....

CHAPTER 1

Trapped!

They were following her, so Gwen walked faster. "I mustn't run," she thought.

It took Gwen 20 minutes to walk home from Avalon High School, but it only took eight if she ran. She knew that because, these days, she ran home every day after school. The four girls always followed her. They insulted her and, sometimes, they pushed her. She heard one of them say something cruel and then, something hard hit her back.

Now she ran. But the girls ran too.

She turned into a **path** behind the school. It went to the town centre. Usually, the girls left her alone in town because there were many people around. Gwen ran quickly down the path, but the **bullies** followed behind her.

She gave a cry of horror when she saw that, today, the path ended at a **locked** gate!

There was a big stone in front of the gate and something **was sticking out** of it. Gwen climbed onto the stone to try to jump over the gate, but she fell.

"Get her!" shouted one of the bullies.

Gwen tried to climb onto the stone again. She **grabbed** the thing to pull herself up. It was hard and cold, like metal. Now, the four girls were right behind her.

The metal thing suddenly moved out of the rock with a strong flash of light. It was a **sword**!

Then, everything went dark and quiet. The hard ground under her feet was now wet and soft. She could smell grass and flowers. Gwen heard a boy laughing not far away. The bullies weren't there any more.

"Where am I?" she thought. "How did I arrive in the countryside?"

CHAPTER 2

A Shock for Gwen

"A few more hours of being a nobody," the boy's voice said. "Then, tomorrow, I'll pull the sword from the stone. And finally, after all these years, I'll get the crown, the castle, the servants, the gold …"

"Now, Arthur … " said another, older, voice.

"Don't forget to call me *King Arthur* tomorrow, Merlin!" said the boy. He laughed arrogantly.

Gwen was surprised to hear the famous names. "It can't be!" she thought. It was dark, but the moon was shining and she was still holding the sword. She looked down at it and suddenly, she understood the significance. "I pulled a sword from a stone!" she thought. "Just like in the legend …"

"Ah, yes," Merlin was saying, "*King Arthur*. I'll try to remember."

"The people of Camelot will shout 'Long live King Arthur' tomorrow!" the boy said. "So **even** an old man like you will remember."

Gwen wasn't only surprised, she was shocked. Arthur was being impertinent to the great wizard Merlin. Gwen knew the legends of King Arthur very well. Arthur's father, King Uther, died when Arthur was a baby. Merlin **hid** the young boy until he was old enough to be king. During this time, many people fought to be King of England after Uther. But, **according to** the legend, only the true king could pull the sword from the stone. And *Gwen* was now holding that sword!

"I must put it in the stone again," she thought, suddenly afraid. But that was impossible. Arthur screamed. "My sword! Where is it? Who's taken it?"

Taking a legendary sword from a wizard and a future king was a bad idea. But getting captured by the wizard and the future king was definitely a worse idea!

CHAPTERS 1-2 ACTIVITIES

1 Write the vowels *a, e, i, o, u* to complete the word in each sentence.

1. A person with a bad memory sometimes f .... rg .... ts things.
2. I scr .... m .... d because I was afraid.
3. It was funny, so I l .... gh .... d.
4. Kangaroos can j .... mp very well.
5. A person with a good memory usually r .... m .... mb .... rs everything.
6. You can cl .... mb mountains.
7. Your friend knows the way, so you should f .... ll .... w her.

2 Match the pictures to the words below.

.... a. **gold** .... b. **grass** .... c. **countryside**

.... d. **crown** .... e. **gate**

Did you know?

People think that the swords from the time of the King Arthur legends, were 7 or 8 kgs, but it's not true. Swords were only between 1.3 kg and 3 kg. Boys learnt how to use swords when they were around seven years old. By the time they were 15, most boys were experts.

3 Write the letter of the correct character(s) next to each quote.

a. The bullies   b. Merlin   c. Gwen   d. Arthur

.... 1. "I'll get the crown, the castle, the servants, the gold …"

.... 2. "I'll try to remember."

.... 3. "Get her!"

.... 4. "Where am I?"

4 Match A and B to make sentences about the story. Then use the number and letter in each pair to find the hidden word and complete the sentence below. The first one is done for you.

A	B
1. The bullies	...1... a. followed Gwen down a path behind the school.
2. Gwen pulled	.... b. the sword was missing.
3. The sword took	.... c. Gwen back to the past.
4. Arthur was	.... d. holding the future King's sword.
5. Gwen knew	.... e. the sword from the stone.
6. Arthur discovered	.... f. arrogant and impertinent to Merlin.
7. Gwen was	.... g. the legends of King Arthur.

	a	b	c	d	e	f	g
1	(d)	k	v	s	d	p	r
2	o	f	u	a	e	n	s
3	b	h	s	c	j	t	v
4	o	i	e	u	a	t	y
5	f	r	m	s	q	w	i
6	j	n	z	t	r	t	b
7	l	m	v	y	i	l	h

The sword in the stone is also called the sword of
d......... ....

CHAPTER 3

Just Like in the Stories

"If I run now, can I escape before they know I'm here?" Gwen thought, as she tried to hide behind a rock. But then, she suddenly stopped at the sound of her name.

"You can come out now, Gwen," said Merlin.

"Of course! Wizards can see through rocks," she thought. This was worse than the bullies catching her after school.

With no other option, she stood up with the sword in her hand. She tried to offer it to Arthur, but it almost fell from her hands.

"There's the thief!" cried Arthur, pointing his finger at Gwen. "Catch him!"

"*Him*?" asked Merlin.

Gwen walked around the rock, pulling the sword. In the moonlight, she could see that Merlin had long white hair and a beard, just like in the stories. He looked like a good man.

Merlin was smiling, but Arthur was furious.

"Get him!" shouted Arthur again, but instead, Merlin **bowed** very low to Gwen. "We've waited for you for years. Long live … "

But Arthur didn't let Merlin finish his sentence. "That's not the King!" he interrupted. "*I'm* the King and that's *my* sword!"

Stand up immediately, Merlin!

Merlin stood up straight again and spoke in a very serious voice. "Only a king can pull the sword from the stone," he said. "We all know that."

"No!" shouted Gwen. "I can't be a king because I'm a girl. I didn't plan to pull the sword from the stone. I was running from some horrible bullies after school … "

"You're a *girl*?" cried Arthur, sounding angrier than before. "*A girl* pulled the sword from the stone? That's even worse!"

CHAPTER 4

A Hard Lesson for Arthur

Arthur went near to Gwen and looked at her face. Now, she could see him clearly. He had light hair and blue eyes, just like hers. His face was very similar to hers. But she detested him and now, it was her turn to be angry. "Yes, *a girl* did it, Arthur!" she cried. "What are you going to do about it?"

Arthur looked at Gwen with hate in his eyes.

Put my sword in the stone again!

Gwen **nodded**. "Yes, that's a good idea. Let's do that."

She tried to move the sword. It wasn't heavy but it was very **sharp**. "Er … can you help me move it, please?" she asked.

"You said that it was easy," said Arthur, **unkindly**.

"The true king pulls the sword from the stone," said Merlin. "Nobody said anything about putting it in the stone again."

"But you said *I* was going to be king!" Arthur cried, sounding like a small child. "Do something, Merlin!"

"In a way, you're king too, Arthur," said Merlin. "Gwen is your distant family from …" he paused and **winked** at Gwen, "a place very far away. She left home very suddenly."

"Merlin knows who I am!" Gwen thought. "He really is a magic wizard, just like in the legends about him."

"But she's a *girl*!" Arthur said. "And girls can't be kings."

This was true, and Gwen didn't want to be king, or even queen. But Arthur's attitude was making her angry again. He was nothing like the Arthur in the legends.

"And **spoilt** little boys can't be kings," she answered. "Kings must be reasonable, just and responsible! You're clearly none of those things!"

"Don't fight," said Merlin, trying to calm the situation.

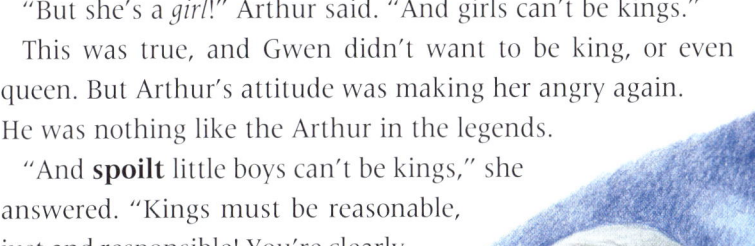

I have an idea.

A few hours later, Gwen looked completely different. She had a new, shorter haircut and she was wearing some of Arthur's clothes. Arthur sat by the window, looking at her, and saying nothing. He was not happy.

However, Merlin had something else to say to young Arthur, and he was shocked when he heard it.

"She'll need a **squire**," said Merlin. "You're not the King, Arthur, but this way, you can always be near the King."

"A squire! I'm not a *squire*!" Arthur protested. "I should have a crown on my head and expensive clothes. I should carry a big sword and have servants and … "

"If you want to wear a crown so much," said Merlin, "you can dress as a girl called Gwen and marry your new king."

The look on Arthur's face was pure horror!

"But," Gwen said, "in the legends, King Arthur was married to Guinevere!"

She stopped. Merlin smiled and said, "Yes."

Gwen was thinking intensely. Her name, Gwen, was short for 'Guinevere', although she never used that name. Was that only a coincidence? She assumed that Merlin knew this too.

"Merlin, listen to me carefully," she said in a very serious voice. "I'm not marrying him! He's horrible and spoilt."

"Don't worry! I'm not marrying *you*!" Arthur answered.

"Excellent! You both agree on something!" said Merlin with a smile. "That's already a good sign! You'll be a great squire, Arthur. I predict that our lives are going to be very interesting and different soon!"

CHAPTERS 3-4 ACTIVITIES

1 Match the sentence to the correct picture. Pay attention to the words in bold.

1. He is **waiting** for his friend.
2. The woman is walking **carefully**.
3. The woman is **angry**.
4. The man has got a **beard**.
5. The boy's books are **heavy**.
6. The girl is **carrying** an umbrella.

2 Use the words below to complete the sentences.

marry   spoke   short for   stood up   reasonable   predict

1. I .... it will rain tomorrow.
2. My name is Becky. It's .... Rebecca.
3. I don't want to .... anyone until I'm 35.
4. The King came into the room and everyone ....
5. Doing homework for five hours every night isn't ....
6. I waited for silence before I ....

3 **What happened next? Circle the correct answer.**

a. Arthur bowed to Gwen.
b. Gwen bowed to Arthur.
c. Arthur discovered Gwen was a girl.

a. Arthur pointed at Gwen.
b. Merlin used magic to make Gwen come out from behind the rock.
c. Gwen thought "Merlin knows who I am."

a. Gwen gave the sword to Arthur.
b. Gwen got a new haircut.
c. Arthur got a new squire.

a. Gwen got angry with Arthur.
b. Merlin made a suggestion.
c. Arthur took the sword from Gwen.

4 **What might Gwen think? Tick (✓) the correct answers.**

.... 1. Merlin knows everything about me!
.... 2. Arthur and I will be good friends one day.
.... 3. Arthur will be a great king.
.... 4. I can't be king!
.... 5. I'm so happy Arthur is going to be my squire!

In the UK until recently, the eldest son of the king was the first in line to the throne. A woman became queen only if there were no sons. In 2013, the law changed and now, the eldest child of the monarch, boy or girl, can become the next ruler.

CHAPTER 5

King Arthur Goes to Camelot

The next morning, Merlin disappeared early with the sword. When he returned, he told Gwen and Arthur it was time for 'the ceremony'.

"What ceremony?" asked Gwen. But Merlin didn't explain. "Come with me," he said. "We're returning to the stone."

Lots of people were waiting when they arrived. The first thing Gwen **noticed** was that the sword was back in the stone.

"Go to the stone," Merlin told her. "You know what you must do."

The people were very quiet as Gwen went to the stone and pulled the sword from it easily. "King Arthur!" Merlin exclaimed. All the people, except Arthur, bowed and shouted, "Long live King Arthur!"

That day, they began their long journey by horse to the king's castle, Camelot. Every morning, Arthur tried to teach Gwen how to use the sword.

"This is a **waste** of time," Arthur protested. "You're not **brave** enough to use the sword. And kings usually teach their squires, not the other way around."

"One day, maybe you'll find Gwen has things to teach you," Merlin told Arthur.

It took five days to arrive at Camelot. The news of the new king travelled fast, and the people were excited and curious to see him. All along the route, they gave them food and places to stay.

By the time they arrived at Camelot, Gwen was brave enough to hold the sword, but that was all. She couldn't fight with it, and her arms and shoulders hurt from practising so much.

At Camelot, thousands of people watched the coronation of Gwen. At dinner, she sat at the top table with Merlin and other important people. She felt bad, because Arthur was sitting at a corner table with the servants.

After the ceremony, Merlin took her to the Great Lake. A hand appeared out of the water. It was holding a sword made of gold and silver.

"This is Excalibur," said Merlin, "the magical sword of the Lady of the Lake. It's yours now, your majesty."

Excalibur was **lighter** than her old sword and easy to use and soon, Gwen could fight as well as Arthur. She was very happy, but Arthur wasn't happy at all! Gwen gave him her sword from the stone, but it didn't help.

"Thank you, *Queen* Arthur," he said, unkindly. Now, when they practised sword fighting, Gwen believed Arthur was really fighting her. And Merlin was not around to assist her. He was busy with 'a mission in another place'.

CHAPTER 6

A Surprising Visitor

One day, a woman came to visit the King.

"Good day, I'm Morgana," she said. "Don't you recognise me? I'm your **half-sister**. Our father was King Uther."

Gwen knew that name from the legends, but she couldn't remember why. Arthur opened his eyes **wide** with surprise, but he was behind Morgana, so she didn't notice.

"It's been a very long time," said Morgana.

"Nobody told me about you," Gwen told her, also very surprised.

"I was four years old when Merlin took you away," said Morgana. "I didn't understand why he didn't take me, too."

Gwen didn't know what to say. She also thought it was unjust.

"But I understood when I was older," Morgana added. "Only the future *king* was in danger after our father died. I was just a *girl*, so I wasn't in danger. I wasn't important at all. There was no *Queen Morgana* in their plans."

"That sounds right to me," said Arthur, from behind her. "I can understand that!"

"Who said that?" Morgana cried, angrily turning around and looking at Arthur. She looked at him for some time.

"Hmmm … your squire is extremely impertinent!" she said, finally.

Gwen was afraid. Why was Morgana looking at Arthur for so long? Did she recognise her half-brother? Did she notice something was wrong?

"Yes, he *is* very impertinent!" said Gwen, quickly. "I must find a better servant. Please leave the room, Squire!"

Arthur stood up and left the room, constantly watching Morgana's face.

Gwen tried to act natural. "Come, Morgana," she said. "Let's get to know each other now. We'll take a walk around the castle. I'm sure you'll have many **memories** of this place."

They walked around the castle and Morgana remembered many things from her infancy. She looked happy to be there again.

"I stood here on this balcony and watched Merlin take you away," she said, when they arrived at the top of one of the **towers**. She had a strange expression on her face. Suddenly, she looked hostile and dangerous. Morgana turned around to Gwen. "And now, Queen Morgana will stand on this balcony and watch you leave *again*!" she cried, and she pushed Gwen with all her **strength**.

Gwen fell back and Morgana followed, ready to push her one more time.

CHAPTERS 5-6 ACTIVITIES

1 **Complete the puzzle. Use the clues to help you.**

Across
3. Playing with fire is very ....
5. The most important people sit at the .... table.
8. We want to leave at six o'clock, so we must wake up ....
9. I can't wait for the party. I'm very ....
10. I want to .... to Venice because I didn't see everything the first time.

Down
1. Nobody .... the actress because she wore glasses and a big hat.
2. I broke my arm and it really ....
4. It's very .... to see snow in the desert.
6. The .... from London to Barcelona is two hours by plane.
7. I .... bad because you couldn't come to the party.

Did You Know? Hundreds of years ago, salt was a very expensive luxury. It was always put on the top table near the king and other important people.

2 **Which sentences in the text give you the information below? Copy the sentences.**

1. The people were silent as Gwen went to the stone.
   ....

2. Arthur didn't like teaching Gwen to use a sword.
   ....

3. The people were interested to see the new king.
   ....

4. Gwen felt sorry for Arthur when he sat with the servants.
   ....

5. Gwen learnt to be a good fighter with Excalibur.
   ....

3 **Put the events in order according to the story. Then match the sentences to the pictures below.**

.... a. Morgana pushed Gwen.
.... b. Gwen got a new sword from the lake.
.... c. Gwen pulled the sword from the stone again.
.... d. Arthur's half-sister arrived at Camelot.
.... e. Morgana looked at Arthur for some time.

CHAPTER 7

A Terrible Dragon

At that moment, Arthur entered the balcony and Morgana turned around to look at him. That gave Gwen enough time to stand up, but Morgana saw her and tried to push her to the floor again.

"Use your sword!" Arthur cried.

He threw Excalibur across the balcony and Gwen took it.

Morgana laughed. "Do you think you can fight *me*?" she cried. She began saying words in a strange language and moving her hands in the air. "Try now!"

As Gwen and Arthur were watching, Morgana's body started to grow bigger and bigger until she almost filled the balcony. Her body turned green and wings grew from her back. Her neck became longer, her eyes turned yellow and her mouth filled with teeth.

"A dragon!" Gwen screamed.

Gwen was afraid, but excited to see a real-life dragon, too. This was another thing from the Arthur legends! But what was she going to do about it?

The dragon flew over the wall of the balcony and away from the castle. Then, it turned around and **breathed** fire at Arthur and Gwen. They threw themselves to the floor and the fire **just missed** them.

From above, Morgana shouted, "Let's see who's not important *now*!"

"We must go inside the castle!" shouted Arthur. "She wants to kill us!" They ran from the balcony and down the stairs to the main hall. Frustrated, Morgana breathed more fire at the stone walls of the castle. Then, she burnt some trees in the garden, too!

CHAPTER 8

A Dangerous Situation

Arthur and Gwen watched from the windows. Morgana was burning things for fun. This was a very dangerous situation.

"So now we have two queens," said Arthur. He smiled for the first time. "And you won't believe it, but I prefer the first one!"

Over the next few days, villagers and farmers came to the castle from all over the country to **complain** about the terrible dragon.

"It ate all my animals in the night!" shouted one farmer.

"I woke in the middle of the night and my farm was on fire!" cried another. "My sheep and cows are dead and now **I have nothing left**!"

My house! My house!

The dragon burnt the words "Arthur must go!" into the fields. It destroyed entire villages and the people were very frightened.

The villagers talked about the situation. "The dragon is angry because of the new king," they said. "Is Arthur bringing bad luck?"

Why can't he kill the dragon?

"What can I do?" thought Gwen. "I need Merlin's help. But where is he?"

Gwen had no option. She consulted her only friend – Arthur. At first, he was arrogant.

"A *real* king could **deal with** dragons," he said.

"If you don't want to help me, then, I must stop Morgana alone," Gwen said.

"Look," said Arthur. "There's only one thing we can do."

"*We*?" Gwen repeated.

"Well, you can't do this alone," he said.

"Why? Because I'm a *girl*?" asked Gwen, still angry.

"No!" said Arthur. "Because that dragon is dangerous. We must kill it."

"But how?" asked Gwen.

"Together," he answered.

CHAPTERS 7-8 ACTIVITIES

1 **Circle the correct word under each picture.**

fun / frightened

neck / wings

inside / above

destroyed / dead

stairs / floor

2 **The words in bold are in the wrong sentences. Write them next to the correct sentences.**

1. We **threw** to the USA. ....
2. I **grew** the ball to the dog. ....
3. The trees **flew** taller than the house. ....
4. The smell of the fresh flowers **became** the room. ....
5. It **filled** difficult to see as the sun disappeared. ....

At the time of this story, about 90% of the population of England lived in villages. The village usually included a lord's house, a group of small houses and fields. The lord rented the houses and sections of the fields to farmers to grow food. The farmers also paid taxes to the lord.

3 **Match the pictures to the sentences below.**

.... 1. Morgana changed into a dragon.
.... 2. The villagers talked about the dragon.
.... 3. Morgana breathed fire at the castle.
.... 4. The dragon destroyed villages.

4 **Tick (✓) the sentences true (T) or false (F).**

		T	F
1	Gwen was afraid of the dragon.		
2	Morgana burnt the castle walls.		
3	Some people thought the dragon was good luck.		
4	Gwen wanted to ask Arthur for help.		
5	Arthur's feelings about Gwen started to change.		

CHAPTER 9

A Conversation Between Two Friends

The next day, Gwen and Arthur rode their horses from one burnt village to another on their way to find the dragon. They couldn't believe the destruction all around. They spent many hours together and started to talk about their lives.

After some time, Gwen told Arthur about the bullies at school.

"Do you think you could deal with them now?" Arthur asked. "Maybe you are stronger because of your experience here."

Then, Gwen remembered. She was on her way to fight a dragon! "*Of course* I can deal with the bullies now!" she answered.

Another time, Gwen told Arthur about the King Arthur legends. "The King's **knights** sat at a round table, so everyone was **equal**," she said. "There was no top table. He was a great king."

"You mean *she* was a great king," Arthur said, sadly. "You'll also have a round table and do great things. I believe that now."

Gwen felt bad for Arthur, and didn't know how to answer this.

I don't know, Arthur.

Soon, they arrived at a village near the mountains. Smoke was coming from some houses and others were still burning.

"The dragon came from those mountains," a woman told them. "And it returned to them."

Great! We found the dragon!

It took a long time to arrive at the mountains. They saw a big cave with black burn marks at the entrance. But it was clear the dragon wasn't in the cave.

"We can hide and wait," said Gwen. "Morgana will return and I'll try to talk to her. But you must hide, Arthur. She mustn't see you."

They hid in two different parts of the cave and waited. It was cold and Gwen's back and legs hurt from the uncomfortable space. But she wasn't cold for long.

Suddenly, the dragon entered and the cave was very hot.

Gwen was afraid, but she stood up. "Hello, Morgana," she said. The dragon looked at her and opened its mouth, ready to breathe fire at Gwen.

"I just want to talk to you," said Gwen. "I know you're furious, but you can't destroy entire villages and hurt innocent people. We must find a way to agree and make peace."

"Do you bring a sword to talk about peace?" the dragon **roared**. "You're an enemy, not a friend!"

Morgana breathed fire at Gwen and only just missed her. The dragon's throat turned red with more fire and it opened its mouth to do it again. Behind the dragon's back, Arthur got up silently from his corner and ran towards the dragon, with his sword held high. He knew he must save Gwen!

CHAPTER 10

Hard to Be a Girl

Arthur used all his force and attacked the dragon's leg with his sword. The sword entered the stone floor. The dragon roared with pain. It turned and breathed fire at Arthur, and there wasn't a place to hide.

While the dragon **was facing** Arthur, Gwen used Excalibur to cut off its head!

Finally, the dragon was dead and they were **safe**!

"Gwen! You saved me!" Arthur said.

"Well, you tried to save me too," she replied. "But it's so sad she's dead."

"What?" said Arthur. "Morgana tried to kill you – I mean us – twice! She was **evil**!"

"She was like that because her life was so unjust," said Gwen. "She suffered because she was a girl."

"What do you mean?" asked Arthur, curiously.

"Why didn't Morgana become Queen when King Uther died?" asked Gwen. "She was older than you. Merlin only **took care of** you, not her. Why was that? That wasn't fair!"

"**You're right**," said Arthur. "It *was* because she was a girl – but that's really a stupid reason! Look at you! *You're* a girl and you've just killed a dragon! Maybe I'll have daughters one day. I hope they'll be brave and strong, like you."

"You're a great squire, Arthur," said Gwen. "Maybe one day you'll be king … "

"It's OK," said Arthur. "You're a great King Arthur – I see that now.

Gwen felt a tear in her eye. "I didn't tell you my full name. My friends and family call me Gwen, but that's short for Guinevere. In the legends, Guinevere was the Queen, Arthur's wife. Those stories are hundreds of years old. They got some things wrong, like who pulled the sword from the stone, but they got one thing right: Arthur and Guinevere were a great team together!"

Suddenly, there was a flash of light and Merlin appeared. "What's happening here?" he said. "A dead dragon! And you two are friends! I was only away a week!"

They told him the entire story, but Gwen had the feeling Merlin already knew everything.

"Look! Didn't you notice that?" Merlin asked and pointed at Arthur's sword. "The sword is back in the stone again!"

CHAPTERS 9-10 ACTIVITIES

1 Circle the words in the flag. Then use the words to complete the sentences below.

reason team rode pain mean fair

1. There are 11 people in a football ....
2. It's not .... that some people work hard but don't earn much money.
3. Do you know what these signs .... ?
4. When I had an ear infection, the .... was very bad.
5. I .... my bike to school today.
6. I know you're angry, but that's no .... to shout.

2 Tick (✓) the sentences logical (L) or illogical (I). Pay attention to the words in bold.

	L	I
1 Countries **make peace** by fighting.		
2 It's **uncomfortable** sitting on small stones.		
3 I can't walk because my **throat** hurts.		
4 There are **tears** in your eyes when you cry.		
5 He **got up** from the chair.		

In the 12th century, the round table became an important part of the story of King Arthur. There is an imitation of the round table in Winchester Castle in Hampshire, England, from about the year 1250.

3 Match A to B to make sentences about the story with the word *but*.

A
1. They found the dragon's cave,
2. Gwen tried to talk to Morgana,
3. Gwen said, "I know you're furious,
4. The dragon tried to kill Gwen,
5. They explained everything to Merlin,

but

B
...... a. she didn't want to listen.
...... b. Arthur saved her.
...... c. he probably already knew.
...... d. you can't destroy entire villages."
...... e. the dragon wasn't there.

4 Who did it? Write the character's name next to each sentence. You can use the same character more than once.

Merlin  Arthur  Gwen  Dragon

1. Who didn't want to make peace? ....
2. Who hurt the dragon's leg? ....
3. Who cut off the dragon's head? ....
4. Who was sad that Morgana was dead? ....
5. Who changed his / he`r opinion about girls? ....
6. Who admitted a secret? ....
7. Who pretended to be surprised? ....

CHAPTER 11

The Sword in the Stone

It was true. Arthur's sword was sticking out of the ground, next to the dragon's body.

"Oh … it doesn't mean anything now!" said Arthur. "It's just an ordinary sword."

"… in the stone," said Gwen. She understood everything now. "It's the Sword in the Stone again. That's very significant."

"Only the true king can pull the sword from the stone," said Merlin. "Everybody knows that."

"But what does that mean?" asked Arthur. "Does Gwen have to pull my sword from the stone and give it to me every time?"

"Well, that depends on her," answered Merlin. "Gwen, now that you understand the significance of pulling the sword from the stone, do you want to do it again or are you ready to return to your old life?"

As he spoke, a strange thing happened. The cave wall and the dragon disappeared and the three of them were next to a path. They heard the sound of feet running on hard ground and someone shouted, "Get her!"

Gwen's face went pale. She recognised that voice.

"I brought you here to teach Arthur an important lesson. He was young and arrogant before," Merlin explained. "Are you ready to be King now, Arthur? Pull the sword from the stone and you will be King Arthur."

"Really?" Arthur's eyes shone and he immediately extended his hand to take the sword. But Merlin didn't look happy.

Arthur looked at Gwen and then stopped.

"It's not important if I'm ready or not. Gwen **deserves** to be king. I can't send her back there to the bullies."

The path started to **fade** and the sounds of voices grew quieter. Merlin was smiling now.

Gwen **took a deep breath**. "No, Arthur," she said. "You must follow your heart. You *are* ready to be king – you just showed that. The old Arthur didn't think of others, only himself. But you wanted to protect me, like a true king."

Arthur **shook his head**. "No, I can't do this to you."

Gwen smiled. "I can do this," she said, with emotion in her voice. "I just killed a dragon, after all!"

She pointed at the sword. "Pull it from the stone, Arthur!"

CHAPTER 12

The End of the Problem

The sounds of running grew louder again and they could clearly see the path now. This time, Arthur pulled the sword and it moved out easily.

"Take Excalibur too," Gwen told Arthur. "It belongs to you now."

"Goodbye, Guinevere," said Merlin. "You will always be a part of history and legend."

"Goodbye, Queen Arthur, and thank you for the round table idea! And I know you can deal with those bullies!" called Arthur, **encouragingly**.

And then, he and Merlin disappeared.

Gwen walked down the path and noticed she was back in her school uniform and trainers. The gate was still locked, but the stone wasn't there.

At that moment, the bullies **caught up with** Gwen.

"I've got you!" one of them cried. She put her hand on Gwen's shoulder.

"No! I've got *you*, you mean!" cried Gwen.

Gwen grabbed a long stick of wood and moved it in the air like a sword. One of the girls tried to take it from Gwen, but she was too quick. Another girl tried to do the same thing, but Gwen hit her hand with the stick. The girl cried in pain and put her fingers in her mouth.

Suddenly, the bullies looked like small children, Gwen thought. And Gwen wasn't afraid of them any more! She put the stick down and in a strong, clear voice, she said, "Go home! This stops today."

The girls looked at each other in shock, and then, they turned and ran.

That day was the end of Gwen's problems with the bullies at Avalon High School.

EPILOGUE

Gwen's memories of her experience in Camelot faded over time. She read and re-read the legends of King Arthur and Guinevere. According to these legends, Arthur never died. Instead, the Lady of the Lake took him to an island called Avalon.

One day, Gwen was in class when the teacher said, "Please welcome our new student from …"

She looked at the light-haired, blue-eyed boy standing at the front of the class. "Where did you say you were from, Arthur?"

"I didn't say," the boy answered.

"Well, anyway," said the teacher. "Welcome to Avalon High School, Arthur. Find a seat."

"There's one here," said Gwen, pointing to the empty seat beside her.

"Thank you, Gwen," said Arthur.

"Oh, have you two met?" asked the teacher.

"Not for a few hundred years," said Gwen, smiling. "But I know we are going to be great friends, in the future!"

CHAPTERS 11-12 AND EPILOGUE ACTIVITIES

1 **Put the letters on the crowns in the correct order to make words and then write the words under the correct pictures. The first letter of the word is always in white.**

2 **Use the words below to complete the sentences.**

welcomed   went pale   belong to   ordinary   met   showed

1. We .... at school and became friends immediately.
2. I wear .... clothes for school because we haven't got a uniform.
3. My parents .... my new friend and invited him to dinner.
4. I found a phone on the bus. Does it .... you?
5. The dog barked and .... its teeth.
6. She felt ill and her face ....

3 Choose the correct answer.

1. Why was the sword in the stone important?
   a. Arthur couldn't pull it from the stone.
   b. Gwen couldn't pull it from the stone.
   c. Pulling it from the stone could change everything.
2. At first, how did Arthur feel about becoming king?
   a. excited
   b. afraid
   c. He didn't want Gwen to be angry with him.
3. How did Gwen feel about the bullies?
   a. She felt stronger than them because of her training with Arthur.
   b. She didn't care about them any more.
   c. She wanted to be friends with them.
4. What happened when the new boy started school?
   a. Gwen didn't like him.
   b. The teacher forgot where he was from.
   c. He and Gwen recognised each other.

4 Who or what do the words in bold refer to? Write the words next to each sentence.

1. **It** was sticking out of the ground. ....
2. I brought **you** here to teach Arthur an important lesson. ....
3. "You can deal with **them**!" called Arthur. ....
4. One of the girls tried to take **it** from Gwen, but she was too quick.
   ....
5. The Lady of the Lake took **him** to an island called Avalon.
   ....

Did you know?

There is a real sword in a stone near Siena in Tuscany, Italy. The sword is 900 years old and people believe St Galgano Guicolotti put it there after an angel told him to become a holy man.

GLOSSARY

English	Castellano	Català
according to	según	segons
bowed	hizo una reverencia	va fer una reverència
brave	valiente	valenta
breathed	echó, lanzó	va treure
bullies	acosadoras	assetjadores
caught up with	alcanzaron a	van agafar / atrapar
complain	quejarse	queixar-se
deal with	ocuparse / encargarse de	encarregar-se de, enfrontar-se a
deserves	se merece	mereix
encouragingly	de modo alentador	de manera encoratjadora
equal	iguales	iguals
even	incluso	fins i tot
evil	malvada	malvada
fade	desvanecerse	esvair-se
grabbed	agarró	va agafar(-se a)
half-sister	media hermana	germanastra
hid	(se) escondió	(es) va amagar
I have nothing left	no me queda nada	no em queda res
just missed	pasó rozando	va passar just pel costat
knights	caballeros	cavallers
lighter	más ligera	més lleugera
locked	cerrada con candado	tancada (amb cadenat)
memories	recuerdos	records
nodded	asintió con la cabeza	va fer que sí amb el cap

GLOSSARY

English	Euskara	Galego
according to	-en arabera	segundo
bowed	agurra egin zion	fixo unha reverencia
brave	ausart	valente, afouto
breathed	bota zuen	botou, lanzou
bullies	jazarle(ak)	acosadoras
caught up with	-engana heldu ziren	acadaron a
complain	kexatu	queixarse
deal with	-z kargu egin, arduratu	ocuparse / encargarse de
deserves	merezi du	merécese
encouragingly	adore-emaile	de maneira alentadora
equal	berdin	iguais
even	baita... ere	mesmo, incluso
evil	donge, gaizto	malvada
fade	itzaltzen, desagertzen	esvaecerse
grabbed	eutsi zion	agarrou
half-sister	ahizpaorde	media irmá
hid	ezkutatu zuen	agochou(se)
I have nothing left	ez zait ezer gelditzen	non me queda nada
just missed	ondo-ondotik pasa zitzaien	pasou rozando
knights	zaldun(ak)	cabaleiros
lighter	arinago	máis lixeira
locked	giltzarrapodun	pechada con cadeado
memories	oroitzapen(ak)	lembranzas, recordos
nodded	buruarekin baietsi zuen	asentiu coa cabeza

GLOSSARY

English	Castellano	Català
noticed	se dio cuenta (de)	va veure, es va adonar (de)
path	camino, sendero	camí, sender
roared	rugió	va rugir / bramar
safe	a salvo	fora de perill
sharp	afilada	afilada
shook his head	movió la cabeza	va fer que no amb el cap
spoilt	consentidos, mimados	consentits, aviciats
squire	escudero	escuder
strength	fuerza	força
sword	espada	espasa
took a deep breath	respiró hondo	va respirar profundament
took care of	cuidó de	va cuidar, es va ocupar de
towers	torres	torres
unkindly	con poca amabilidad	amb poca amabilitat
was facing	se enfrentaba a	s'enfrontava a
was sticking out	sobresalía	sobresortia
waste	pérdida	pèrdua
wide	mucho, como platos	molt, de bat a bat
winked	guiñó el ojo	va fer l'ullet
You're right	Tienes razón	Tens raó

GLOSSARY

English	Euskara	Galego
noticed	ohartu zen	se deu / deuse conta (de)
path	bidexka	camiño, carreiro
roared	marru egin zuen	ruxiu
safe	salbu, onik	a salvo
sharp	zorrotz	afiada
shook his head	burua mugitu zuen	moveu a cabeza
spoilt	mizke hazitako	consentidos, mecosos
squire	ezkutari	escudeiro
strength	indar	forza
sword	ezpata	espada
took a deep breath	sakon arnas hartu zuen	respirou fondo
took care of	-z arduratu zen	coidou de
towers	dorre(ak)	torres
unkindly	adeitasunik gabe	con pouca amabilidade
was facing	aurre egiten ari zela	se enfrontaba a
was sticking out	ateratzen zen	sobresaía
waste	galtze	perda
wide	guztiz, erabat	moito, como pratos
winked	keinu egin zion	chiscou o ollo
You're right	Arrazoi duzu	Levas / Tes razón

CROSS-CURRICULAR FOCUS
Where Do Legends Come From?

KING ARTHUR – LEGEND OR HISTORY?

There are more films, books and poems about King Arthur than any other English king. But historians can't find any documents to prove he was a real person. Some people think a person like Arthur lived in the 5th or 6th centuries. At that time, England was under Roman **rule** and there was a Roman soldier-king called Riothamus. His name means 'supreme king'. He crossed the sea to fight in France to protect England from invaders. People were afraid of wars and violence and they wanted to believe the King could save them. It's possible that stories about Riothamus developed into legends about King Arthur.

The stories, as we know them now, began over 800 years ago. A British writer called Geoffrey of Monmouth wrote a part-fiction, part-history book in the 12th century called *The History of the Kings of Britain*. He **borrowed** ideas and names from earlier legends. One of his stories was about a boy called Arthur, son of Uther. According to this story, Arthur became king when he was 15 years old. He and Merlin fought against the Scots, the Irish and other people in different lands. When he was away, his son, Mordred, took his throne. Arthur returned to fight him, but Mordred **injured** him and he went to the island of Avalon to **recover**, but he never returned and no one ever saw him again or found his body.

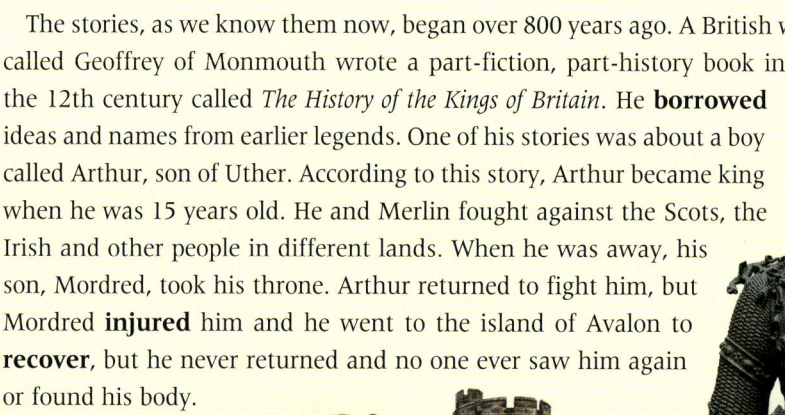

rule	dominio	domini	jabetzako lur	dominio
borrowed	adoptó, se apropió de	va adoptar / apropiar-se	eskuratu, -z jabetu	adoptou, apropiouse de
injured	hirió	va ferir	zauritu, kolpatu	feriu
recover	recuperarse	recuperar-se	suspertu, indarberritu	recuperarse

1 Tick (✓) the sentences true (T) or false (F).

	T	F
1 Arthur is a popular character in literature.		
2 Documents show Arthur was a real person in the 5th century.		
3 Arthur and Merlin fought wars against the Romans.		
4 Riothamus wrote the first stories about the legend of King Arthur.		
5 In the stories, Arthur left England to fight different people.		
6 Arthur never returned from Avalon.		

2 Find six words from the text in the puzzle. Then use them to complete the sentences below.

s	i	n	v	a	d	e	r	s	l
o	p	e	i	w	v	a	d	r	d
l	r	b	o	r	r	o	w	e	d
d	o	p	r	o	s	e	v	f	r
i	v	r	e	t	u	r	n	e	d
e	e	e	n	e	a	o	r	a	t
r	o	t	h	r	o	n	e	d	o

1. Historians can't .... Arthur existed.
2. Riothamus was a .... and a king.
3. Riothamus fought in France to protect England against ....
4. Geoffrey of Monmouth .... stories about the kings of Britain.
5. Mordred sat on the .... when Arthur was away.
6. Arthur went to Avalon, but he never ....

WHERE DID THE IDEA OF DRAGONS COME FROM?

Dragons have existed in stories in many cultures for centuries. In European legends, dragons are **huge**, fire-breathing **lizards** with wings, but in Asia they are more like snakes and have no wings. They also appear in writings from the Greek and Sumerian civilisations **dating as far back as** 2100 BC.

In the Middle Ages, people probably believed dragons were real, because they were in the Bible. For example, in the Book of Job, chapter 41, there are stories about a monster with flames coming from its mouth and smoke coming from its nose. It also had very hard skin-like armour. People believed that dragons were connected with Satan and the fire represented Hell. For every evil dragon, there was a Christian hero like Saint George. He lived around the 4th century and historians think he was a real soldier. According to legend, he killed a dragon.

There are other explanations for why people believed in dragons. Since the 19th century, we have known about dinosaurs. But people found giant dinosaur bones and **skulls** in China as far back as 2,000 years ago and thought they were dragons. Early explorers travelled from Europe to Asia and Africa. They returned with descriptions of Komodo lizards. These stories encouraged people at that time to believe in dragons.

Today we might not believe in dragons, but their power over our stories continues. You can probably think of lots of films, books and video games with dragons in them!

huge	enormes	enormes	izugarri(ak), ikaragarri(ak)	enormes
lizards	lagartos	llangardaixos	musker(rak)	lagartos
dating as far back as	que se remontan a	que es remunten a	-koa izan	que se remontan a
skulls	cráneos	cranis	garezur(rak)	cranios

CROSS-CURRICULAR FOCUS

3 Choose the correct answer.

1. People in the Middle Ages thought that dragons were **real** / **not real** / **from China**.
2. People in the Middle Ages read about dragons **from Greece** / **in the Bible** / **from China**.
3. A dragon's skin was very **soft** / **hot** / **hard**.
4. Historians think Saint George **was a real soldier** / **killed a dragon** / **explored Asia**.
5. Explorers' stories of **dinosaurs** / **Komodo lizards** / **Saint George** made people believe in dragons too.

4 Find words in the text to match the pictures. Write the words. Then use the words to complete the sentences below.

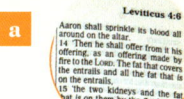  

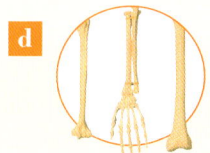 

1. European dragons didn't look like .... because they had legs.
2. European dragons breathed ....
3. Dragons in the .... also breathed smoke from their noses.
4. Dragons also had skin like ....
5. Thousands of years ago, people found .... from dinosaurs.

 **MINI TASK** Search the Internet for information about another legendary creature. Write a few sentences about the information you find.